Bubba's Financial Planner

A guide to lifetime
financial planning for the
unsophisticated, uninformed
and uninterested individual
concerned about his or her
financial future

James Compton

authorHOUSE™

1663 LIBERTY DRIVE, SUITE 200
BLOOMINGTON, INDIANA 47403
(800) 839-8640
WWW.AUTHORHOUSE.COM

First published by AuthorHouse 3/30/2006

ISBN: 1-4208-8956-7 (sc)

Printed in the United States of America
Bloomington, Indiana

This book is printed on acid-free paper.

The information in this book consists of my opinions. I have tried to present an assortment of ideas gleaned from life experiences to help others. Seek professional advice and help with your investments. It will be money well spent.

DEDICATION

I would like to dedicate this book to my wife and daughter who helped me grudgingly with this publication. They do not enjoy studying finance either!

Thanks to Nancy Roberts

Table of Contents

INTRODUCTION

The saying goes that money is the root of all evil; actually it is the root of the tree of our financial life-good or bad. Will your tree bear good fruit or wither and die? Much of how that turns out is up to you.

This publication is not a detailed investment guide nor does it contain all the information on all areas of lifetime finance and investing. It serves as an introduction to help the individual set up a financial plan to get through life successfully. Hopefully you will be stimulated to take control of your finances and take an interest in your financial future. No promise is made that you will become rich. You will gain financial guidance and suggestions that few people receive in school or from their parents. It opens windows that will enlighten you to areas of finance and investing with which you probably feel uncomfortable, and gives you suggestions for further reading to expand your knowledge and confidence. Being financially successful is not that difficult if you set out with a sound plan and stick with it. The most important part of financial planning and investing is to start! The second most difficult part is to stick with it through thick and thin. Every day you hear people say that they are going to invest in the next "hot" stock or as soon as they payoff their vehicle or other debt, but that day never seems to come. Time is in the favor of the investor.

Financial success does not mean that you are independently wealthy. It does mean that you are in control of your finances. This publication is not a retirement planner. Too much is said about retirement and too little about the 40 to 50 years from the time you enter the job force until you retire. If you live these years prudently, retirement will take care of itself.

I have not tried to rely on exact figures or specific current legislation or tax laws, as they will change over time. As I suggest later on, seek out competent advice on these matters from your broker or tax accountant and do not mind paying for the advice; you usually get what your pay for.

Be careful in listening to your friends about investing advice. Much of this is like what you hear from people returning from the casinos. You only hear about the winners, not the losers, much less the true net from the trip. If people won as much as they say they did, why are they wasting their time working for a living?

You may consider yourself an average person with an average income, but do not let that stop you from believing in your financial future. Look at this example from "The Americas Finest Companies Investment Plan" by Mr. Bill Staton. Mr. Theodore Johnson worked for UPS, never making more than $14,000.00 per year, but he invested regularly. At retirement his portfolio was worth $700,000.00 and when he died at age 90 it had grown to $70,000,000.00! Yeah that first million is tough, but it really can snowball after that. You may have no desire to accumulate this kind of wealth, but is shows that anyone can if they start early, stick with their plan, and live within their means. Good parents should want to provide for their family and for their children's potential education after high school.

This guide is to help you establish financial goals and guidelines and serves only as an introduction. There are hundreds of good investment books available in the bookstores or at your local library to increase your knowledge. Most are not necessary and many may prove counter productive as we tend to be our own worst enemy when it comes to money and investing. After establishing a good financial plan, you should only have to review it annually.

It has been said that money is not everything, but I say it is well ahead of whatever is in second place. Whether you like it or not money runs or ruins your life. It is one of the leading causes of divorce and college dropout. Every aspect of your life is affected by money. Shelter, food, transportation, charitable giving, everything you do is bound by financial restraints. You wake up in a home or apartment that you are paying for, take a bath with water you pay for and pay to heat, brush your teeth with a toothbrush and toothpaste you bought, etc, etc, etc. Yes sex is not free; you either pay for contraception or the children. Learning to accept and live within these financial boundaries is the first step to financial success.

Realize as you read about investing that no one knows what stocks, bonds, interest rates, inflation or the economy as a whole will do in the future. They have an opinion just like you. If you read the statistics about the recommendations of most financial planners, investing newsletters, and most mutual funds, you will find that most do not beat the S&P 500 index over an extended period of time. If they are so smart why can't they beat the "market"?

The average person stumbles through life with little or no training beyond how to balance a checkbook. Think back, how much instruction did you receive when you were growing up on financial matters? Are you not investing because you do not feel comfortable about brokers or investing? When we attempt most tasks in life we have a plan, an outline, a "to do" list to guide us to our goal, yet most people attack their financial life in fits and starts if at all. Should we not have a plan for the one aspect of life that has the greatest affect on us? Many of the following suggestions may be perceived as silly, but these ideas establish a mind-set towards money that is necessary if you are to be financially successful. Either you control your finances or they will control you!

Do not worry about keeping up with the Jonses, or the neighbor next door with all the new toys and driveway jewelry; he is probably dead broke. This brings up one of the first principles; you must learn to live within your income. If everyone in our society were financially successful and lived within his or her means we all would be much better off. If we all provided for our own retirements we would not need social security and would have that money to invest for ourselves and leave to our heirs, not to donate to someone else!

Before going forward, let me state a maxim that I believe you should understand before reading this or any other financial book, or before taking any advice. There are no "right" decisions only "informed" decisions. You can plan all day and everything comes out all wrong. That is called life. If you do not try at all, that is called stupid!

At the end of each section, lines are provided for you to make notes for your financial plans.

_____

_____

_____

_____

_____

_____

_____

_____

_____

_____

_____

_____

_____

_____

_____

_____

_____

_____

_____

_____

_____

INCOME

The first area we need to discuss is income. If you are a millionaire you probably wasted your money on this publication. However, if you are, more likely, one of the millions of working, average citizens you live off your weekly, biweekly, monthly income. During your life you may have job changes, bonuses, lay-offs, your income may rise or fall but two facts in your financial life that you need to understand are: 1) pay yourself first (savings/investments) 2) budgets do not work.

Starting with your income, if you cannot live or are not willing to accept your present income level, remember that you can do something about it! You can change jobs, take on a second job, start a business on the side, or advance your education to get a better job. America is the land of opportunity and you are only limited by your own ambitions.

FIRST STEPS

It is a good idea, as a starting place, to do a monthly spending/income analysis, just to see where you stand financially and where your money is going. Write down all present incomes and deduct all "fixed" expenses such as rent, utilities, car payments, insurance and food. How much is remaining? At this point you have to decide whether the amount left over is acceptable, or if you need to increase income or reduce spending. Evaluation of your checkbook allows you to find spending habits that could be modified to allow you to save that money. I do not remember the exact figures, but a couple went to an investment advisor for help. They could not find any money to invest yet they realized that they needed to start investing. The investment advisor, analyzing their checkbook, asked them what the daily check for $10.00 to $20.00 was for. They stated that they went to work in the same vehicle and stopped at a high priced coffee shop for 2 cups of fancy coffee, 2 bagels and a newspaper every morning. The advisor informed them that (assuming 20 workdays per month average) that amounted to $200.00 to $240.00 per month. He suggested they subscribe to the paper, make their coffee at home and bring their bagel from home. That would free up $100.00 to $150.00 per month to invest. Sometimes it is that simple; you just cannot see it.

Now let us address some areas in which you can improve your financial situation. First comes your checking and savings accounts. Your banking accounts should reflect your financial needs. Break down the use of your income into the following areas.

A. Monthly bills: Utilities, time payments, rent or mortgage payments, and other fixed living expenses.
B. Savings for large lump sum payments: car insurance, Christmas, taxes, etc.
C. Back up savings for emergencies: CD's, Money market account, savings account, extra money in checking account.
D. Investments: primarily stocks and bonds.

Your bank account, along with your credit history are the foundations of your finances. How much are you paying in fees at your bank? Are your checks free? All services that you pay for are wasted money. The first step is to build up your balance or find a bank that provides free checking and free checks. If you are paying $10.00 (for example) a month for a checking account and $10.00 per month for check printing, that would equal $240.00 per year in fees/charges. You would have to have $4,800.00 invested at 5% to get the return of $240.00 per year. Shop around for a bank that offers the most services for the smallest balance when starting out. Many banks, for larger balances offer free safety deposit boxes, free cashier's checks, lower rates on loans and higher rates on CD's. Usually this is fair because the poor tend to be bad money managers, higher credit risks and have lower balances in their accounts. Remember the bank makes it's money by loaning out your deposits. I know you are thinking I do not have the extra thousands of dollars to step up to these accounts. Few people do when starting out but if you start saving towards that first goal you will eventually reach it. To reach this goal, set aside a designated amount from your pay in a regular savings account. To build up extra money in your regular checking account, try rounding your checks to the next higher dollar amount when you subtract from the previous balance. This allows you to build up a safety cushion over time. When you do your monthly bank statement simply subtract the balance you calculate from the balance in your checkbook to find out how much "extra" money you have in your account. Don't spend it, leave it there as a cushion. You might think I could invest that money, but believe me the sense of security of knowing you have a couple of thousand extra dollars in your checking account is worth the small amount of interest lost, and some banks pay a small amount of interest on checking accounts so all is not lost. Eventually you have your own overdraft protection built in. With the advent of debit cards this may become difficult to do. In place of this you may have to set aside regular payments into your money market account for protection and to build up your extra money.

The prime moneymaker for most banks is fees. They just love for you to overdraft or break any of the other rules so they can charge you fees. One bank offered their "sub-prime" customers (those with small balances and low incomes) free checking accounts. Considering what we discussed above, why would a bank do this? They knew that those customers were usually the worst money managers and would probably overdraft their accounts. They were correct and collected almost a billion dollars in overdraft fees that year.

Let us assume you have your feet on the ground and have built up a little nest egg in your checking account, and have accumulated enough money to get checking accounts with low or no fees. You will already feel better about yourself and your finances and slowly the perceived financial strain lessens. The next two steps regarding your bank accounts are up to you. Realistically you do not need both accounts, but it makes life easy to have both accounts.

First, establish a savings for rainy day/emergency expenses in a money market account. Do this by establishing the account then set aside a set amount per paycheck to contribute to this account. The money market checking account has two advantages. It draws interest and you have immediate access to the money in an emergency by simply writing a check. There are limitations on the number of checks written per month, but this should not be a problem as this money is only for emergencies and not for "stuff", therefore you should not write checks on a regular basis. When you use funds from this account you have to pay it back. This borrowing from yourself saves you interest. You are simply borrowing from yourself rather than a credit card or the bank. You will lose less interest on the money than the amount of interest you would have paid other sources of credit. It also allows you flexibility in your repayment schedule.

When you have built up a larger balance in this account through monthly contributions, it is a good idea to "park" some of it in a "CD" (certificate of deposit). CD's pay more interest than the money market account and you still have access to that money, should the need arise through cashing in the CD or borrowing against the CD at your bank, usually at a reduced rate.

One rule of thumb is to keep two to three months worth of gross income in the money market account and CD's for emergencies. Yes, this may seem like a lot, but in life a lot can happen, and though you may not want to spend your hardearned savings it beats the heck out of having to borrow the money in an emergency. The bank might not want to loan you money if you just lost your job!

The next step is to establish a passbook savings account to set aside money for those large expenses that regularly occur on a quarterly, semiannual, or annual basis. Almost everyone will say, "I cannot afford to save that much money." Well, they are going to have to pay the bills one way or the other, why not set aside a little at a time and have the money to pay the bills when they come due? Obviously, most people finance these bills paying out interest that could have been saved.

What expenses come under this heading are strictly based on your family needs. We all have different needs and wants. Just for example I will use the following categories that affect most families. Car insurance – if you pay semiannually you will pay significantly less for coverage, again saving money. Vacation savings, savings for Christmas, college savings for children, and if your house is paid for you will need to set aside money for insurance and taxes and maintenance.

In the example below, let us assume you are paid twice monthly. You must set up a simple ledger to keep up with savings for each category and have a cumulative total column so you can reconcile with your bank statement.

Date	Car Insurance $100/ck	Vacation $100/ck	Christmas $50/ck	College $25/ck	Total $275/ck
1/1/05	100.00	100.00	50.00	25.00	275.00
1/15/05	200.00	200.00	100.00	50.00	550.00
2/1/05	300.00	300.00	150.00	75.00	825.00

These dollar amounts and categories are for example only, not recommendations for you.

When the bill comes due, you transfer the money to your checking account and write a check for the bill. You accomplish several goals with this system. First, it forces you to save for necessary/mandatory bills and prevents you from blowing that money on other "stuff". You have built financial security by not only having the money to pay the bill on time you have saved interest and have built another nest egg that would be available in life or death circumstances.

Let me interject at this point another important fact for most people. For now I will name it Compton's law. It states that the majority of people, rich or poor, will spend every dime in their checkbook between paychecks. If you do not set aside for these needed expenses you will blow the money on something else.

One item you may want to include in this category is income tax. If you come up short every year, either have your withholding increased at your job, or set aside money as you go to pay your taxes. After all, death and taxes are inevitable.

Now we will assume that you have your financial base in place and working for you. You have control of your expenses and hopefully have curtailed your borrowing and saved a lot in interest. Plus you have the financial security to sleep without worrying about how you are going to pay the bills.

_____

_____

_____

_____

_____

_____

_____

_____

_____

_____

_____

_____

_____

_____

_____

_____

_____

_____

_____

_____

TEACHING CHILDREN
ABOUT MONEY

Here is a good place to mention educating your children about financial responsibility. Starting early in their life, give them an allowance and make them stick within that allowance by not giving in to more purchases. As they grow, increase their allowance including such items as clothing purchases and eventually gas money for their car, and again make them stick within their budget, i.e. out of gas, out of money – you walk! This will help them learn how to budget money. Around high school age it is time to start training with a checking account to go along with their allowance. I do not recommend credit cards for children; the temptation and lack of understanding of the risks are above their heads.

_____

_____

_____

_____

_____

_____

_____

INSURANCE

Before we enter investing, let us briefly cover some related financial areas that affect all of us. Insurance is an area that confuses many people and many dollars are wasted on unnecessary insurance while you may not be getting the coverage you really need. Each family has different needs when it comes to insurance coverage. Medical, automobile, renters, homeowners, life and long term care are some of the common types of coverage you may be confronted with. There are a lot of good agents with good intentions, but remember they make a living SELLING insurance. You can get insurance poor very quick. The money you are paying for insurance could have been invested in your long-term savings.

Automobile insurance: A minimum of liability coverage is required in most states to legally operate a vehicle. In addition you can purchase collision insurance, small medical coverage for occupants of the vehicle, and comprehensive coverage to cover freak accidents such as hail damage. One option that is usually available for a small increase in premium is to step up to a $100,000.00/$300,000.00/$50,000.00, or similar higher coverage. At the current price of vehicles this is well worth the money.

If you have a collision, your insurance will not buy you a new car. It will repair it or total it and give you the amount it is worth in the wholesale market. Is it worth it to pay for collision and comprehensive on a ten year old vehicle? Why not save that money? If you have a loan on your vehicle the bank will require full coverage, not to protect you but to protect their car while you are driving it and paying it off.

Renter's insurance: Starting out in life you may feel that you have few personal possessions. Stop and add up what it would cost you, new prices, to replace all of your clothing, and other possessions. You will be surprised at how much the total will be. For a small fee, usually in the $75.00 to $150.00 range you can get coverage on your possessions. You cannot control the person smoking in bed next door to you. It is an inexpensive investment in peace of mind.

Homeowner's insurance: Be sure you have a good agent that knows your needs. Do their recommendations make sense? Check out what is commonly called "replacement" insurance. For a relatively small increase in premium cost this coverage will guarantee replacement of all depreciated items such as an old refrigerator up to specified limits. Understand what is included in the policy and what you are paying for.

Medical coverage: This is by far the most important insurance you can obtain. This should be one of the primary concerns when entering the job market. You can work, save and then have an illness and the doctors and hospital will get it all. The only advice you can really give on health insurance is purchase the best you can afford. See your human resources department and make sure you understand your insurance and other health benefits before you need them.

Other insurance related items: Although not "insurance" many companies offer medical savings accounts, (FSA's), and day care savings accounts. These are two of the few remaining tax breaks for the average working person. These are wonderful plans that help you to save and smooth out your out of pocket expenses for drugs and medical care and for child care. The plans are managed in different ways, but in a nut shell you decide how much money you will need for out of pocket medical expenses and how much money you will need for child care over the year and have that amount divided by the number of pay checks you receive in a year. This amount is placed in your savings accounts and you can file on those plans, when you have an expense, to get your money back. Many are offering debit cards to access those funds. These plans save you taxes as you do not pay taxes on the money set aside and they force you to save for these mandatory expenses. These are truly tax-free, not tax-deferred plans. Again, see your human resources department for details and understand them completely before participating. The medical savings account will become more important in the future as companies shift more financial responsibility for medical costs to the employee.

Long-term care insurance is available independently and through many employers. Before you sign up for this insurance be sure you understand why you are signing up. Long term care pays, in most cases, for your care in a nursing home or similar facility, and for at home care if you are disabled and not able to work but not in such health that a nursing home is required. If you have few assets do not pour money into this insurance. What you are really protecting is your assets. However, if you have built up a significant nest egg and do not want to go broke paying for health care, and wish to preserve that money for your wife, husband, or children this is a good idea. Usually if you are well off, this allows you to easily pay for nursing home care and allow your family to continue with a normal lifestyle.

Life insurance: Life insurance has a good safe ring to it, but is it necessary in your life setting? First of all why do you need life insurance? The purposes of life insurance are to pay off all residual debts of your estate, to provide for your family upon your untimely demise and to protect your assets for your family at the time of your death. It would take a book to describe all of the types of life insurance offered for sale today. However, we can break it down in to two basic types, whole life and term life insurance. Under the whole life plan you pay for a predetermined time for a specified amount of coverage. Under most plans you can borrow against any cash value and the policy cannot be cancelled unless you miss payments. In whole life insurance you, in most cases, build up a "cash value" that you can borrow from or "cash in' the policy and receive that amount. This sounds good until you look at the fees involved and the rate of return. This is not a good way to invest. Unless you buy enough life insurance to cover all of your debts and death expenses, why buy any at all? And if you purchase a lot of insurance, you are losing the time and investment value of the money you are paying the insurance company. Think hard about the benefits before purchasing a policy. One instance that whole life might be worth the money is if you are the kind of person that will not save and invest, at least it will leave your family with something.

Term life is usually the best value for the average person. It is frequently available inexpensively at your place of employment. Term life is almost self-explanatory. For a fee, an insurance company agrees to cover you with a fixed dollar amount for a specified "term", usually one year. Term life gets more expensive as you get older as your risk of dying becomes greater, but if you have your financial house in order you should need less insurance at that time as you should be better off financially.

There are many other types of policies available, just be sure if you decide to purchase insurance you evaluate why you are purchasing the policy, and how much coverage do you really need. Any money given to the insurance company could have been invested for you.

_____

_____

_____

_____

_____

_____

_____

_____

_____

_____

_____

_____

_____

_____

ACCESS TO CAPITAL: (LOANS)

Almost everyone needs to borrow money during their lifetime. There are many sources from which to borrow money. You can borrow from a bank, a savings and loan, a credit union, your 401k plan, credit cards, whole life insurance, margin account or, in most states, against your home equity. If you have CD's, you can borrow against them at a reduced rate. This is simply a secured loan. For most people credit cards are the most expensive way to borrow. The only difference between armed robbery and credit cards is that with credit cards no weapon is used and you volunteer to be robbed monthly! For example a customer who had a $10,000.00 balance on a credit card with a 16% interest rate and who makes the 2% minimum monthly payment will take more than 40 years to pay off the balance (assuming nothing else is ever charged on the card) and would cost $19,329.00 in interest! There is talk that the government may even get involved with credit cards. On the average each American family has about 8 credit cards, no wonder we have a problem.

The second worst source of credit is a cash advance loan at one of the local loan shops. These have horrible rates and fees and are strictly for suckers.

Mortgage loans are probably the average person's most important investment in their lifetime. You should try to make a significant down payment, shop around for the best terms, fees and interest rates and take the shortest pay out period you can afford. The difference in the amount of interest you pay on a 20 versus a 30 year loan is significant. Usually the difference in the monthly payment is relatively small.

For example borrow $50,000.00 at 7% for 30 years and you will pay out a total of $132,076.80. The same loan for 20 years will cost you a total of $100,372.80. A difference of $31,704.00! The difference in the monthly loan payments would be $366.88 vs 418.22 or $51.34 per month. The difference in payments is usually so small that if it really makes that much difference to you financially, you probably should not make the loan. This all comes back to the simple fact, buy a home you can afford. The mortgage payment becomes a fixed expense for a very long time, and unless your income increases dramatically, the home of your dreams may become the nightmare that prevents you from enjoying the rest of your life.

When purchasing a home, do not forget that the larger the home the larger the taxes, upkeep expenses, insurance and utility bills.

As a suggestion to help you with all loan shopping, go to a bookstore and obtain a copy of a bankers P&I (payment and interest) book. This publication has tables that lay out the term of the loan, amount of loan and monthly payments, and these books are cheap to purchase. Do not forget on a mortgage loan you will also be responsible for an escrow account to pay for taxes and insurance, which adds a significant amount to the monthly payment.

Many people choose to take out home equity loans. These can be relatively cheap methods to borrow money. However if you are borrowing money to pay off credit card debt, it will do no good unless you lose the credit cards! You will just end up deeper in debt.

Your credit is your best asset. If you pay on time (preferably early) and are prudent with your borrowing you will build up a good line of credit over the years should you need it. To check on your credit you can access any of the three bureaus by phone, writing or on line.

Equifax
P. O. Box 740241
Atlanta, GA 30374-0241
(800) 685-1111
www.equifax.com

Experian
P. O. Box 2104
Allen, TX 75013-2104
(888) 397 3742
www.experian.com

Trans Union
P. O. Box 2000
Chester, PA 19022-20000
(800) 888-4213
www.tuc.com

Hint: Some banks will give better rates to customers that have the loan payments automatically deducted from their checking account. This also has the advantage that you will never have a late payment.
One last statement on loans, never co-sign another person's loan unless you are fully prepared to pay the loan off yourself. If a person needs a co-signer that tells you they have no credit or bad credit.

_____

_____

_____

_____

_____

_____

_____

_____

_____

_____

JOB RELATED BENEFITS

For the average worker some of the most important financial decisions they will make in life are decisions related to their job benefits. When job hunting, remember that benefits are actually a part of your take home pay and equally as important. Retirement plans, 401k (or similar plans), medical savings/day care plans, life and health insurance, stock options, stock purchase plans and disability insurance are some of the commonly offered benefits. Spend some time making good decisions regarding your benefits. Most HR departments will be glad to help you through the maze so you can take advantage of the benefits that you need.

Retirement plans come in so many variations that only the basics will be covered. The retirement plan I am referring to is one in which the employer contributes to your plan, this is not the 401K plan. It may be a plan where your employer contributes a specified amount to a funded plan in your name or to a pension plan. Pension plans are plans where contributions are made, usually by the employer, to a fund, not in your name, that, upon your meeting the requirements for retirement under that plan, a formula is used usually taking in consideration years of service, scale of pay and other factors to calculate a monthly pay out. Such plans, for example are those of railroad workers, teachers, and state or federal employees. Most pension plans guarantee you will never go broke but you will never be rich. In most cases you will need to set aside other savings for a comfortable retirement.

In a funded plan, your employer and in some cases you, contribute to a plan that holds the money in your name. In most cases you have to work for a set number of years to be "vested", which means qualified to claim the funds your employer contributed. Be sure you understand this vesting before changing jobs. It may cost you a lot of money to change jobs if you lose the unvested amount in your account. Also in funded plans, if you do change jobs, make sure you "roll over" the funds you are qualified for to another qualified account. You need to involve your stockbroker or the institution to which you wish to transfer these funds to coordinate the transfer. If you receive a check in your name you will usually be responsible for paying income taxes on the full amount in that tax year and you will also, in most cases, be hit with a tax penalty if you access these funds before age 59½.

Another plan to help you set aside funds for your retirement is a 401k or similar plan. In these plans you are allowed to set aside tax deferred funds, lowering the income taxes you pay, into a plan that usually has several investment choices. The government sets the limits on how much you can contribute, currently around $14,000.00 and allows "catch up" contributions for those over fifty, but the government changes it frequently depending on the mood of Congress. Tax deferred does not mean you will never pay income taxes on the money, it means that you will be allowed to invest this money and allow it to grow tax free until you start to take it out. At that point you will be taxed on the money as regular income. This allows you to make more money on your investment as you have more money working for you. The general consensus is that at retirement, you will be making less money and thus paying less taxes and possibly at a lower rate.

A proposed "Roth 401K" is in the works in the Federal Government. Under this plan you would contribute after tax dollars to a retirement plan, your employer may or may not match any of these funds just like the current 401K plans. The advantage is that you would be able to withdraw your money tax-free when you meet the standards set by the government. For many this would be preferable to the current 401K plan. The money grows tax deferred just like the current 401K plan.

Understanding how tax deferred accounts will help you on your current income taxes is simple. Assume you make $40,000.00 per year and contribute 10% ($4,000.00) to the 401K plan. You will only be responsible for taxes on $36,000.00 and the $4,000.00 will grow tax deferred.

In many 401K plans the employer will match in some manner up to a limit your contributions. If you do nothing else, at least contribute up to the limit of the employers matching funds. This is free money; you cannot beat that as an investment!

A lot of confusion arises in how to invest these 401K funds. In some plans the only choice is the employer's stock. Be very careful in how much you invest in these "one stock" plans as they can lead to disaster. You truly have all your eggs in one basket (remember Enron?). In contrast to this type of plan most employers offer a variety of investment options that include some of the following choices. A money market fund, bond funds, equity (stock) funds, and balanced funds, and the company's stock. In evaluating the risk/reward of the above options obviously the company's stock may offer the highest potential reward but has the highest risk. The money market fund should have the lowest risk as far as loss of principal. The "balanced funds" are usually a mix of money market funds, bonds and stocks. Two things for the novice to remember about these options are: do not let the term "bond fund" give you a false sense of security as these can be very volatile as far as loss of principal. They are not the same as actually owning the bond yourself. Secondly, when evaluating risk levels, do not forget inflation. Your principal may not be lost in a money market fund, but over time inflation will erode it significantly. If you are making 6% on the funds in the money market fund and inflation is running 3%, you are only making 3% return on your money. Economists refer to this as the "real rate of return".

As a starting point your 401K, or similar plan, should provide you with the investment performance of each of the investment options over the past 1, 3, 5 and 10 years. All stock and bond funds will have up and down years; you are interested in the long term performance. In bond funds you are more focused on capital preservation and income. In the cash or money market portion you are interested in capital preservation and income.

For a middle-aged worker a general conservative recommendation would be 50% stocks, 40% bonds and 10% in fixed income investments. As you approach retirement it is prudent to shift from stocks into income funds. Not that you want to delete stocks totally from your portfolio but to reduce the risk that the day you retire the bottom falls out of the market because of some happening such as 9/11! Close to retirement you might have a mix containing only 20% stocks in your 401K plan.

Your retirement and 401K plan at your place of employment might offer such fantastic potential that you do not need to set aside additional funds for retirement. In most cases this is not true and you will need to have additional investments to guarantee adequate income and security in your retirement years.

One factor that most financial experts and financial planning books focus on to excess is retirement. If you will invest, and live your financial life prudently, that is live within your means; retirement will take care of itself. Remember most of us have 40 to 60 working years between the end of our education and potential retirement years. We need to focus on these years that make up the majority of our lives. As stated before, most of us start out broke; it is where you go from there that counts. You will not become financially secure overnight. One of the biggest faults that most people have is the urge to buy something every time they have built up a little nest egg. Money begets money by compounding. You have to leave it alone to let it grow.

_____

_____

_____

_____

_____

_____

_____

_____

_____

_____

FINANCING CHILDREN'S EDUCATION

I hope you plan to set aside funds to help with your children's education. On the average, a child with a college education will earn double what a person without a college education earns in a lifetime. That is a lot, and it is one of the best investments you can make in your children. This does not necessarily mean a conventional college education. There are many technical and medical fields with wonderful employment potential and financial reward, but they require training and education. In today's world it takes training and education to excel or even to qualify for employment in most fields and is mandatory for employment in many fields.

As far as financing their education, before you sign on to any "state sponsored" plans, read the fine print very closely. Many are very poor investments, cover nothing but direct educational expenses and should your child not decide to seek higher education may turn out to be real losers. Counsel with someone that thoroughly understands all ramifications of the plan before investing. At worst, they are better than doing nothing.

Other plans such as a 529 or gifts to minors plan are available. Before starting such a plan see an investment professional and understand all the positive and negative points of each plan before investing. Under the uniform gift to minors act, the child has the right to use the funds for anything they wish when they reach legal age. This is about the time their hormones kick in and a trip to Mexico or a new car might look more appealing than college.

An alternative method is to invest in your name using, usually, mutual funds and when the child is ready for college make gifts of these funds to them for college expenses. This way you control the money to the last second. Again, see your broker or CPA for help in this area. This method, having the money in your name, may also help the child obtain other grants or scholarships, as they will not have the money in their name.

PAY OFF YOUR HOME EARLY?

You have established yourself financially, are setting aside savings, and decide it would be a good idea to pay off your home early. Maybe you receive an inheritance or large bonus. Many financial experts claim this is the best use of your money. First let me state that it is a better idea to pay off your home in place of blowing the money. Most people propose to pay off the loan by making extra payments towards the principal. I believe we can pay off the loan as early or earlier and use the money more intelligently.

Let us suppose you are paying all of your extra income towards the note on your home with the hope of being out of debt ten years sooner than the original term. Again, not a bad idea for the average person must have the home paid for before they can retire. But life happens. Maybe the economy falls in to a deep recession, housing prices fall (remember Houston, Texas in the 1980's?), and you lose your job. You may have to walk away from the home or sell it at a fire sale price to salvage your credit. Either way you lose the home and possibly your credit rating. One of your family could come down with a serious illness and you need the money for that purpose. Fill in the blank with your disaster. The bank will not give you back any of the extra money you have paid towards the loan, nor do they pay you interest or dividends on the money. They will, assuming that you have good credit and a job after the disaster happens to you, loan you money against the home, of course with interest.

If you are really determined to pay off your loan early, set the money aside in investments and do not use it for any other purpose. If and when the amount equals the loan pay off amount, you will have the choice to use it for that purpose. Up until that date you have earned interest or dividends on your investments and it may save your life in an emergency. I believe <u>you</u> should always maintain control of your money.

INVESTING

To understand investing you must understand some basic economics. One of the prime factors that directly affects your savings but goes unseen is inflation. Inflation is simply the increase in the price of goods and services over time. An annual inflation rate of 3 to 4% goes almost unnoticed to the average person. When the prices of goods and services increase the purchasing power of your income decreases. For example, if you receive a 3% "raise" in your salary at work and inflation is running 3%, then you actually did not receive any increase in your salary. You just kept up with inflation, which means you will be able to purchase the same amount of "stuff" as you did last year. In other words you did not come out ahead. In some cases because of the way your pay increase affects your income taxes you may come out behind!

Look at inflation from the investment side. If you are receiving 3% on your passbook savings and inflation is running at 4% you came out 1% behind in purchasing power. You actually lost money. Economists refer to the impact of inflation on investments at the real rate of return. In other words, the amount of return with inflation factored into the equation. For example if inflation is running 8% and you are earning 10% on your investments or if inflation is running 3% and you are earning 5%, you really came out with the same (2%) increase in purchasing power on your investments.

To demonstrate the effects of inflation if prices rise at a 3% rate per year, items you purchase today that cost $1,000.00 will cost over

$1,300.00 in 10 years, and will cost over $1,800.00 in 20 years. This is why you need your money to grow over time.

The only time inflation really can help you is if you borrow money, although the interest rate charged by most institutions factors in some inflation protection. Every year that you repay a loan the money you pay back to the institution is worth less in purchasing power.

The opposite of inflation is deflation. We have not suffered from deflation since the depression. In deflation, you are earning less and selling your goods and services for less. Cash is king. The value of your money increases. Sounds good unless you have a loan. The farmers in the depression were trying to pay back loans on their farms that were fixed. Each year the value of their produce decreased and it became harder for them to make payments. Overall, economists agree that a little inflation (2 to 4%) is needed to "grease" the wheels of the economy. One place where it has the greatest impact on the individual is in retirement. Unless you are reinvesting some of your savings to grow your principal, you have less purchasing power each year. This will have a greater impact on our economy as people live longer. We will see more working seniors trying to make up the difference in their income from the affects of inflation.

EQUITIES

"Equities" is another term for stocks. Stock is the fractional ownership in a company. Stock is sold to raise capital for the company to initiate, expand or simply carry on business. Stocks are not complicated. Some of the details are, but you do not need to be a stock expert to make money in the market. In this publication we will deal with the stocks that are represented on the primary stock exchanges and reported in any of the large papers that report investing news, and stock tables.

When a company is started it "incorporates". This incorporation is the birth of the company. At that point the company takes on many legal powers of an individual. It can conduct business, write checks, borrow money, sell stocks and bonds, and purchase real estate to name a few. One of the primary reasons for incorporation is to limit liability of the owners. The owners are the persons who purchase the stock of the company. The company can be sued, but the owners of the stock are limited in liability to the amount they paid for their stock. In other words, the individual stockowners cannot be sued for actions of the company. Obviously in this day and time this is an important factor in business.

The sale of stock allows individuals to accumulate large amounts of capital to start or enlarge a business that they might not be able to access through loans or sale of bonds. When a company "goes public" in an "IPO" (initial public offering) it arranges the sale of it's stock through one of the investment houses. The persons selling the stock, the proposed company and the investment house (in America) have to meet certain standards to sell stock to the public. Just because they meet these standards and are allowed to sell stock does not in any way mean they are good investments.

You read daily of "Blue Chip" or .Com (Dot Com) and other abbreviations to describe general categories in which companies may be grouped. I will briefly give a basic description of the terms you may hear on the news. The term Blue Chip refers to established companies, usually those that have proven themselves over time to have a sound business plan. .Com and E-Commerce refer to companies that in some way use the internet or software for their primary business model. Another common term you will hear is Index and Index Funds.

An index is a ruler or guideline that is comprised of companies that do business in the same general category or in some other manner are related. A common example is the S&P 500 index. This index is made up of 500 Blue Chip companies that are commonly traded on the open market and represent a cross section of American business. Each day the individual stocks of that index go up, down or stay the same. The index is calculated using a formula that takes all of these changes into account to give a figure that simply shows that the index went up in value, stayed the same or decreased in value compared with past index figures.

What good are indexes? They are simply a ruler to give the individual an idea of the market movement and to let the individual investor measure the performance of their investments against the market. There are many different indexes that represent all different areas of business endeavor. If you pay close attention you will frequently see days where the Dow 30 may increase and the S&P 500 may decrease.

Indexes do not as a rule move in tandem. In the long term it is hard for the individual investor to beat the Dow 30 or the S&P 500 index.

To compare your investment returns, see how much your investments grew over the year, not counting money invested during the year, to the Dow 30 or the S&P 500 index. Traditionally over long periods of time the market will return 6 to 10%.

What exactly is a .Com company and why are they so volatile? Volatility refers to the large price swings in stock price. First let us look at a computer software company that represents many of these companies. Most traditional Blue Chip companies are composed of "sticks and bricks". This refers to the fact that they own physical assets such as buildings, real estate, trucks, manufacturing plants, and other "real" assets. This ownership of real property over the broad market gives them a base value, they own stuff. On top of these assets is any additional value of their product and brand name. The brand name may be the largest asset of the company. For example there are Coke and Pepsi. Opposed to this are the software companies and .Com companies. The only real asset they posses is an idea that might be represented on a computer disc. An entrepreneur forms a company around this idea. What real value do these companies have? None except the POTENTIAL value inherent in their idea. They hope that they can market that idea to another company or to the consumer. Microsoft sells such software to companies and individuals. It started out small but was able to gain market share faster that its competitors therefore has become one of the primary software vendors.

Why do these .Com companies have such a potential for wealth? Remember that most of these companies are selling an idea on a disc. It may cost several million to develop that idea and produce the first disc, but how much does the second disc cost to produce? Next to nothing! Look at the potential. These companies do not have to tie up millions or billions of dollars in production and distribution equipment. They simply subcontract out the copying of their disc. The prime costs will be advertising, marketing and distribution.

The only problem is, if you can come up with an idea, so can anyone else; and their idea may be better or they may market it better and you are toast. Easy come easy go as they say. These companies, at least initially, usually have only one idea to market. There are no other product lines to support them if their idea flops. As an investor, this makes these companies very, very risky at best. Ask Bill Gates if he is not afraid of another company coming up with a better idea and crushing Microsoft. It could happen.

As an investor, if you purchase any of these stocks in the IPO stage, just consider it gambling. Yes, if you guess correctly they have unlimited potential, but the majority of them flop. If you are an average investor, you do not have the money to blow on these stocks and lack the access to the inside information to make an informed decision about their potential. You have worked hard for the money you have to invest, don't blow it!

At this point, you are probably asking, "Why purchase stocks at all? I like to feel my money is safe in the savings account at the bank. First, remember how inflation erodes the purchasing power of our money over time? Second, look at this example from Bill Staton's "The Americas Finest Companies Investment Plan". If you had invested $1.00 in each of the three following investments in 1801 where would you be in 1992? Taxes were not taken into account, and are not usually taken into account on projections as they change over time and each person has a different tax situation.

$1.00 invested in stocks would be worth $3,050.000.00
$1.00 invested in short-term government bonds would be worth
$2,934.03
$1.00 invested in long term government bonds would be worth
$6,620.00

Do the math! Yes the stock market fluctuates over the years (i.e. the depression) but look at the difference in the ultimate potential reward. The movement of stock prices has been compared to a person walking up the stairs with a yo-yo. The yo-yo goes up and down but progressively gains altitude as it goes up the stairs. The prime factor to take into account is that the average wage earner cannot contribute enough to their savings account to add up to a significant amount of money over their lifetime. Your only hope in having a significant nest egg is by investing at least a portion of your portfolio in stocks.

Why do stock prices fluctuate? To begin with we need to understand how stocks are valued in the marketplace. A stock is only worth what another person is willing to pay for it at any given time. Just like a used car. Ever wonder where the prices come from that are reported in the newspaper? These are the recordings of the sales of stocks and their prices during that business day. Frequently reported statistics include the high and low price over the past 365 days, closing price for that particular day, (this means the price paid for the last trade on that business day), the dividend yield in %, and the dividend in dollar amounts and the price to earnings ratio (P/E ratio). Back to our initial question of who sets the price of stock. The buying public and corporate investors (such as mutual funds and insurance companies) set the price. If someone believes that a stock is priced low they will purchase it, if they hold stocks and believe that the price is too low and may not recover soon they might sell, or they might believe the stock is overpriced and they have made a good profit and sell to lock in that profit. This process is accomplished through a broker. The broker finds someone willing to sell if you want to buy or someone to buy if you want to sell. Your trade is recorded on the "tape" and becomes part of that day's statistics. Currently you have 3 business days to pay for the stock after you ask your broker to purchase it for you. The process in the background of how stock is purchased and sold is beyond the scope of this publication and has no significant affect on the small investor. If you are interested, many good books are available on the subject.

The physical way the market functions is being changed almost daily with upgrades in technology, the internet and E-Commerce. As stated before this process does not affect the small investor. An investor is interested in accumulating shares of stock in companies that will, through business expansion, raising dividends, repurchase of stock or through other methods increase the value of their stock over time. If you invest in a company that is growing through these processes it will be reflected in the company's stock price over time.

The massive daily selling and buying of stocks confuses people. Why would you want to sell a stock? Mutual funds and individuals buy and sell stocks to "rebalance" their portfolio, they may see a "hot" stock that they need money to purchase, many are "Day Traders" that try to make a profit primarily on small movements in stock prices.

Before you decide to become a day trader realize that around 70% of all day traders lose money, and of those that do profit, the majority make only a small return on their money. They pay to buy and to sell and pay taxes on any profits. This is strictly legalized gambling for the small investor. Making money over time on good investments is not hard. If you receive a hot stock tip or a "cold call" from some broker you have never met, ignore them! Buy stocks and mutual funds you have investigated, let your earnings compound, and do not give up your profits to your broker and Uncle Sam. There are hundreds of good blue chip companies in which to invest. Why buy junk?

When is a good time to invest? Now! No one knows what will happen in the economy or in the world tomorrow. You cannot reap the benefits unless you are in the market. If you read the statistics about individual stocks you will see that they make major price increases on the average of three days out of the year. How do you expect to know which three days to invest? Many are afraid they will lose their money in the market, which in the short term is a very real possibility. When stock prices go down, look at it as a sale. Do you run to the store and stock up on Cokes when they go up fifty cents per bottle or when they go down fifty cents per bottle? Why should you treat good stocks differently? Take advantage of the sales to stock up with more shares, assuming that the company is still a sound investment.

You have to take the emotions out of investing to succeed and this is truly the hardest part of investing. You may have heard of the monkey dart method of investing. This theory supposes you give a monkey a dart and let him throw it at the stock listings from the newspaper and buy the stocks that the dart lands on. A silly way of stating random selection of stocks. For several years the Wall Street Journal ran a contest between financial experts and random selection and it was about a 50/50 outcome on whom selected the best stocks. I do not recommend either method. Do a little research, use common sense and buy companies with good track records. Analyst's opinions are an excellent way to be introduced to new investment opportunities, but take them with a grain of salt. Remember they are just opinions! Before believing any of these opinions, do you know these analysts personally? Do you know the factual long-term record on their recommendations? Do they own any of the stock they are touting? While on this note, do not believe anything you see on the Internet. Why should you believe anything you read on the Internet, placed there by a person using a fictional name for suckers like you? In one study of analyst's recommendations it was found that you would have been better off buying what the analysts recommended to sell that what they recommended to buy.

A very good source of investing information is the Value Line Investment Survey. This is available free at most libraries and two separate publications cover stocks and mutual funds. This reference gives a breakdown of all the statistical information on the company along with an opinion. It is categorized to allow you to seek out they type of company you feel appropriate for you. High yielding companies, growth companies, companies that are currently in vogue are all analyzed and at your fingertips. It also has an address or e-mail address that you can contact to obtain information about the company.

Before you jump in head over heels you must under stand some of the game rules. If you are looking for income most of the high yielding companies are Real estate investment trusts and Royalty trusts. If a stock is not in one of these two categories and has a high dividend yield, there usually is a reason, and not always a good one, or a freak situation that gave a short term burst in the yield. You are usually better off to look to good blue chip companies that have consistently growing dividends. Companies that have a small product line can suffer significant drops in price in an instant. Compared to these small companies are companies such as Proctor and Gamble. They have many products to support their price and if a new toothpaste flops, it will not have a significant impact on the bottom line.

A personal preference of mine is to purchase dividend paying stocks, preferably those that have consistently raised their dividends over the years. Even a small dividend (0.5 to 2%) will help support the stock's price in down times. Believe it or not, dividends make up a significant amount of your portfolio's growth over time.

DRIPS

DRIPS, an acronym for Dividend Re Investment Plans, are an excellent way to take the emotions out of investing. These plans are available from many companies and many allow you to purchase the initial shares of stock direct from the company. These plans are good for the small investor that will research the companies. They allow you to dollar cost average your money over time to purchase shares in a company and reinvest dividends paid to you, sometimes at a discount, to purchase more shares, compounding your investment. They are similar to stock accumulation plans available at most brokerages but have the advantage, usually, of lower fees and lower minimums on purchases, many allowing purchases of $25.00. Most of these plans allow "OCP's" or optional cash purchases on a weekly, monthly or quarterly bases. You can participate in the plans by OCP's or in most instances by having a set amount deducted monthly from your checking account. This is the best way to invest as it takes the emotions out of investing, takes advantage of dollar cost averaging, and forces you to save.

"The DRIP Investor Newsletter" and other sources are available to guide you into knowing which companies are available for DRIP plans and direct purchase DRIP plans. The DRIP plans usually hold your shares in safekeeping and mail you a confirmation when you send in money and send out quarterly statements and 1099's (tax information about your dividends to be filed with you income taxes) at the end of the year.

You can start some plans with as little as $250.00, or in some companies if you will promise to have 10 payments of $25.00 taken automatically from you checking account you can enroll (currently Wal Mart has this type of plan). Don't worry about the taxes, if you are making money, gladly pay the tax! Many of these plans offer IRA plans for those that are qualified.

STOCK BROKERS

The purpose of this book is not to give you all the fine details of each type of investment. It is to simplify and de-mystify investing to make you comfortable with investing. Do not be afraid! It is not hard. If you do not feel comfortable investing on your own, you are not alone. Most people would prefer watching TV or going fishing rather than studying an investment book. If this is the way you feel, seek out a good broker to help you. A good brokerage service will be a source of investing ideas, may offer a monthly stock purchase plan and will take care of your investing and necessary tax records. There are many advantages to using a broker, just make sure you select one that is concerned with your situation.

A good test in the selection of a stockbroker is to walk into the broker's office and say you have some money to invest. Do not tell the broker how much money you have to invest, and do not let the fact that you may not have much money to invest intimidate you. Just say you are looking for a broker to help you with your investments. One of the first questions out of the broker's mouth should be, what is the purpose of your investments and over what period of time do you plan to invest? If the broker does not ask these questions, at a minimum, before suggesting investments than him/her for their time and leave! Other questions should be, is it to buy a new car in 3 years, savings for a home in 10 years, college savings, retirement savings, etc? All of these would be invested in a different manner. Your age, marital status, income and tax situation as well should be added into the equation. Be wary of the broker that discourages you from investing in your company's 401 K plans, and encourages you to invest that money with their brokerage. They may not be looking after your best interest.

Most brokerages offer stocks, mutual funds, bonds, and CD's. When you feel comfortable that you have selected a good broker interested in your goals, set out a plan of monthly investing and stick with it through thick and thin. A good broker will also be a good "hand holder" in the bad times and help keep you on track and prevent you from making "knee jerk" decisions.

Once you have your investment plans in place, either good stocks or mutual funds, forget them and continue to add to them over time. Forget reading the daily stock tables, enjoy life and let your investments take care of themselves. Over the years you will find that you are your own worst enemy. Every time you think you have come up with another bright investing idea, you will usually lose ground. When you sell a good stock that has appreciated in value, both your broker and Uncle Sam will reap part of your profit. The best time to sell a stock is when the company truly starts to make dumb decisions and loses direction or when the inherent business of the company has gone down hill and will remain so for a long time. Without being silly, look at the past. Wagon and harness manufacturers were once big business, then came the automobile and their business was shot no matter how high the quality of their buggy! Also, if you decide to purchase individual stocks, do not expect to make good returns on all of them. You will pick some lemons, just like Warren Buffett, just be willing to learn from your mistakes. A good source of investing ideas can be as simple as looking at the list of stocks on one of the Dow Indexes or the list of the S&P 500 stocks.

A good broker can be your best asset. Use common sense to evaluate their suggestions. Do their suggestions sound reasonable? What were the returns on their investment ideas over the past 5 or 10 years? If you invest in stocks invest with money you know you will not need for the next 7 to 10 years. Another basic rule is to diversify you stock holdings. This means to own many stocks in different business areas, which is hard for the small investor to do. This is the same as saying "Do not put all your eggs in one basket." Traditionally each quarter of the year different business areas will gain more than other areas. You cannot reap the rewards unless you are invested in the market. To familiarize you with some of the general business categories in the marketplace see the list below. It is not a recommendation to buy, just examples that you may be able to recognize.

Basic materials	Sigma Aldrich
Capital Goods	General Electric
Communication Services	AT&T
Consumer Cyclical's	Home Depot
Consumer Staples	Clorox
Energy	Exxonmobil
Financial Services	Bank of America
Health Care	Merck
Technology	Dell Computer
Transportation	Southwest Airlines
Utilities	Atmos Energy
REITs	Weingarten Realty Trust

At this point some of you are asking why I have not mentioned using an on-line (Internet) or discount broker to handle your stock transactions. These services offer cheap trading fees and overall provide good service, however they have drawbacks that can be fatal for the small, or novice investor. With cheap trading fees comes the temptation to trade often which is the nemesis of the small investor. You go from investing, to speculation to on line gambling. It is too easy to turn your investments into on-line gambling. If you have the self-control to avoid these pitfalls then they can be an excellent option to the investor that does not need personal attention, or recommendations from their broker. Too many will see stocks drop, read a bunch of on-line BS about the pending market crash and panic and sell at the time they should be buying (good quality stocks). Most investors get excited as the market rises and buy, then get disgusted when it drops and sell. This is human nature and it is hard to go against that inbred nature.

A simple suggestion for stock selection is to go to a store such as Wal-Mart and walk the shelves. You will find many products by Proctor and Gamble, Golgate, and Gillette. Do you think people will continue to brush their teeth, wash their clothes, and shave? Look at Exxonmobil; will you continue to buy gas? Look at utilities, do you plan to continue to use electricity and/or gas? These are good places to start looking for investment ideas, and then your research starts in earnest.

MUTUAL FUNDS

For the average investor who has no real interest in studying investing and making investment decisions the best investment plan is mutual funds. Let's face it; most people do not get excited about reading a company's annual report. Your broker can set you up with two or three mutual funds that have good track records, through which you can invest on a monthly basis. You can place these funds in Roth, or traditional IRA plans if you are qualified. Investing in mutual funds through a broker allows you to have the money drafted from your checking account making sure you invest, it gives you diversification in your stocks, allows you to take advantage of dollar cost averaging, gives you a concise record for tax purposes, and takes the emotions out of investing.

Exactly what is a mutual fund? They are investment companies originated in the early 20th century that purchase stocks, bonds and other investment instruments, and in turn sell shares to the (usually) small investor thus conveying a fractional ownership in all the companies in that particular fund. For their services the mutual fund companies charge a fee for their management services. Originally they gave the small investor a great advantage because trading fees on stocks were high and it was expensive for the small investor to afford to purchase stocks, much less have enough money to diversify their holdings. You are paying the mutual fund for investment advice, an accurate accounting of your transactions for your records and tax purposes and hopefully their success investing your money. Each mutual fund should offer you a prospectus that states the investment purpose of that fund, and give information on their past performance and usually list the companies owned by the mutual fund with % ownership, list all fees charged by the fund, and explain their investment focus. When fund shopping compare the fund you are investigating with the comparable market index and with other funds with the same investment focus. If the fund did not beat the market index, why not invest in an index fund? Index funds are cheap (usually) because they do not have to hire any one to manage them. They just mirror the index they represent. You will note that few funds beat the comparable, market index over a 5 to 10 year basis.

Currently there are thousands of mutual funds on the market. They vary in focus, to name a few, from Blue Chip, Index funds, Sector funds, balanced funds, etc. A good mutual fund can be an excellent investment for the individual investor, but you have to do your homework just like purchasing individual stocks. Do not assume because they have a good advertisement (nice glossy paper) that they are a good fund. Do your research, evaluate all fees involved, read Value Line mutual fund survey at your library, and evaluate their performance over the last 1,3,5,and 10 years, or over the life of the fund. Literally, some funds are run out of an individual's bedroom! Any one can start a fund, that is why you have to be careful with your research.

The prime disadvantages of mutual funds are, in many cases you are paying fees for a fund that under performs the market, the fund directors are deciding when you have to take a capital gain or loss, and forcing you (in non tax deferred funds) to pay capital gains taxes that you could defer if you owned the individual stock. A fund may have a losing year and you still have to pay capital gains taxes. This is a good place to mention that individual stocks are a form of tax deferred investing. Yes you have to pay taxes on any dividends, but as long as you do not sell, you owe no taxes on the capital gains, which can be significant if you have held a stock for a long period of time.

Many people become "fund-hoppers" always trading funds and purchasing the funds that did best the last quarter. Think about this, you are buying a fund at it's highest price, and last quarter's performance has nothing directly to do with what it will do this quarter. Tech funds had a great 99 but look at 2000! Purchase good funds with good long term track records, dollar cost average and stick with your plan.

You are thinking, but what if I invest at the worst time of the year (when the market peaks for that year)? Follow this classic example of the two brothers. Starting in 1963 an investor with the worst luck ever invested $2,000,00 per year for 10 consecutive years in the market in an S&P Index fund. He invested this money in a lump at the market high each year (the worst time to buy). As of 9/1/00 his total investment of $20,000.00 would have grown to 1,012,170.00. His brother on the other hand was the luckiest investor in the world. He started investing $2,000 per year the year after his brother stopped investing (1973). His luck was so phenomenal that he bought at the market low (best time to purchase) and continued with his investing for 20 years. How did the two compare? As of 9/1/00 the lucky brother's investments (remember he invested $2,000.00 per year for 20 years) would be worth $31.298 less that the unlucky brother. Time is on your side. Forget being able to "time" the market. You can only know in hindsight what was the market high and low for the year. People said years ago that the Dow had broken 3,000. There was no way it could go up so they were getting out of the market. They missed the boom of the 1990's. The best time to start investing is now!

I will repeat this suggestion, as it is probably the best free reference for the small investor. Value Line Investment Survey that covers both mutual funds and individual stocks along with other market information is available free at most public libraries in the reference section.

IRA'S

As there are many types of tax deferred investment methods available I will briefly cover two that are available to most people, the traditional IRA and the Roth IRA. In the traditional IRA you are allowed to deduct the amount invested from your current income lowering your taxes for that year and those funds are invested and grow tax deferred. That means you will eventually pay tax on them when you withdraw them. In the Roth IRA you invest money on which you have paid taxes but are allowed to withdraw the funds tax free once you have met the guidelines of the plan (usually 59 ½ year old). One significant advantage to the Roth is that you can withdraw any of the money you have put into the plan on which taxes were paid at any time without penalty. This is good and bad because the temptation is always there to withdraw your savings. There is a lot of debate on which is the best plan for you. A lot of the decision has to do with your tax situation, and potential future tax situation. The Roth has the advantage in that you can purchase single stocks, mutual funds or a variety of other investments. Seek advice on which plan is best for you. For many people the best plan would be to participate in your employer's 401K plan up the employers "match" limit and place additional investments into a Roth plan with your broker. Every person's situation is different and requires planning on your part to make the best decision. If you do participate in a "traditional" IRA make sure you know exactly how to handle the transfer, or disposal, of these funds if you change brokers or retire. The IRS can punish you with additional taxes and penalties if the transfer or withdrawals are not handled exactly like the government rules and regulations require. Seek professional advice in this area, especially as the laws may change frequently.

_____

_____

_____

_____

_____

_____

_____

_____

_____

_____

_____

_____

_____

_____

_____

_____

_____

_____

_____

_____

_____

OTHER INVESTMENTS

Other investment options you hear mentioned such as options and futures although they do have a purpose in the business community are simply a form of gambling for the small investor. If you want to lose money gambling, go to a casino and at least have a good time for your money.

BONDS

Many types of bonds are available to the investor. Three basic types are U.S. Government, corporate and municipal. United States government bonds are considered the safest form of investment in the world as far as safety of principal (if held to maturity) and as to guarantee of payment of interest. Corporate bonds vary in quality from just under U.S. treasury bonds down to what is referred to as "junk bonds". That term is self-explanatory. Municipal bonds will usually pay less interest than U S Treasuries because they are exempt from U.S and most state income taxes. Bonds in the U.S. traditionally pay interest biannually. The interest rate on individual bonds is adjusted by market forces to reflect the safety of the bonds (higher yield = more risk) and they use the U.S. Treasury bonds as a basis for setting the interest rate. Bonds are rated by such companies as Standard and Poors, and Moodys as to their safety and may be upgraded or downgraded during their lifetime. These changes reflect the perceived ability of the issuing agency or company to pay dividends and return principal to the bondholder. Think of bonds as CD's. You are loaning your money to a company or the government and they are making a promise to pay you semi annual interest payments and return your principal at the end of the term of the bond. If you hold corporate bonds you have first claim on any assets, (next come the preferred stock holders then the common stock holders), should the company fail.

Until later in an individuals investing life, age 50 and up, bonds serve little purpose in the investors portfolio. They offer no significant capital appreciation to the small investor, and usually the real rate of return (interest income minus inflation index) is small. In place of bonds if you has invested in stocks you would hopefully have accumulated a significant investment and if you had not traded stocks over that period of time, you would not have paid taxes on the capital gains. Whereas on bonds, with the exception of most municipal bonds, you would have paid taxes on all of the income (in non-tax deferred accounts). To calculate your true rate of return on bonds you have to take into account any trading fees, taxes you will have to pay on the income and the effect of inflation on both the income and the principal. For example if you had purchased a 30-year government bond for $1,000.00 and inflation ran 5% you would only receive back, after 30 years, approximately $500.00 in principal (in purchasing power) and the "real" interest payment would shrink proportionally. Bonds take on more importance in retirement, as they become, usually, a significant part of your portfolio for income purposes. The Government has recently added inflation-protected bonds to their selection. These help protect you from loss of principal, which is one of the main problems of investing in bonds.

In the class with bonds are many other fixed income instruments to which your broker can introduce you.

_____

_____

_____

_____

_____

RETIREMENT

If you survive your working years, hopefully there is a light at the end of the tunnel and you hope to enjoy the fruits of your labors. As you progress through your working years you should be shifting the focus of your investing from growth stocks, to growth and income stocks and finally towards income stocks and other income instruments. You can also, as mentioned above, include at this point some bonds or other income instruments to increase your monthly income. You also have the choice of purchasing an annuity. If you choose to remain in control of your investments you need to make the shift towards income slowly over the years. If you have a portfolio of growth stocks with low yields at age 65, assuming they have performed well over the years, You are going to take a beating from the tax man if you have to sell all of them at one time and shift into income investments.

Don't forget inflation. You must keep some stocks in your portfolio to provide growth in principal over time, or you will become poorer each year. One option is to use mutual funds for income in retirement. You can purchase funds that focus on income with growth in principal that take care of both problems. You usually start out with less income compared with bonds or other income instruments, but your income grows each year. Your broker can explain how to use these for your retirement portfolio.

Another important factor is Social Security, which is now in debate on what to do to save the plan for future generations. Whatever the outcome you can bet benefits will be reduced. This should be an incentive for you to save more to make up the shortfall that will probably happen. Social Security is not a retirement plan. It was designed as a safety net so no one would starve to death in retirement. Look at your benefit statement that you should receive from the Social Security Administration and see if you can live on your proposed pay out. This should give you some motivation to save for the future.

ANNUITIES

One method many people choose because it is simple and assuming you select a good stable company will provide stable income over your retirement years is an annuity. It would take a book to cover all of the options available in annuities. In its simplest form an annuity is a form of insurance contract that you purchase over time or in a lump sum that invests your money for you and guarantees a set income stream for a designated period of years. They may serve best those who choose to no longer keep up with their portfolios or those facing health problems and wish to have their investments taken care of by someone else. Be sure you understand all the details before purchasing an annuity they can be complex. For many investors a combination of an annuity and a portfolio of stocks and bonds might be the best option.

INHERITANCE

Not all of us will have the problem with excess assets, however, if you have invested over the years and have accumulated a significant nest egg. First, you should have a will made out expressing your wishes on how to divest your assets. A good time to draw up a will is before you have children. If you have a significant nest egg you might seek out an attorney to help you with a trust. Sometimes giving a child a large sum of money at one time is more than they can handle and may do more harm than good. With a trust you can give the child an income stream to help them through life and hopefully not destroy their life.

COLLECTING

Collecting can be a method of having your cake and eating it at the same time, kept in perspective. First of all most modern "collectibles" are made to sell and will have no significant future value. If you are serious about collecting, why not collect something that has a proven tract record as far as increase in value? There are many areas that have proven tract records of increasing in value over the years. Firearms, stamps, coin and bill collections, paintings, antique furniture, to name just a few (properly selected) have proven good investments. If you plan to be a collector, select an area of interest you enjoy, do research and buy the best you can afford. The only problem with collecting is you will seldom want to sell it for retirement needs as you usually fall in love with your collection. It does make a nice heirloom to hand down in the family.

_____

_____

_____

_____

_____

COMPOUNDING

Compounding of interest (and reinvestment of dividends) is one of the wonders of the world; especially in tax deferred accounts. Even Albert Einstein commented on this fact. Look at a few examples to understand this powerful effect. The person who starts saving early and regularly and reinvests their income from their investments reaps these rewards. Missing a few years, especially the early ones, makes a devastating effect. Remember the example of the two brothers mentioned earlier?

Invest $25.00 per month ($300.00 per year) at a 10% annual return x 40 years (age 25 to 65) equals $$132,777.00. With an 8% yield you would end up with $77,716.00. That 2% difference in investment return shows how much impact a small difference in return can make (this includes fees and other expenses that rob you of your final return).

Another example: If you invested only $2,000.00 in an IRA at age 16 and never invested another dime and it is compounded at 10% per year for the 49 years you would have accumulated $213,437.00, again at 8% you would have $86,854.00.

Here is a good place to introduce the "Rule of 72". This is a method of approximating how long it would take to double your money at a certain interest rate. To calculate that period of time, divide 72 by the interest rate of your investment. For example, if you invested $5,000.00 at 6% it would take you approximately 12 years to double your investment (i.e. to $10,000.00).

You may wonder how to compound your income (dividends) from stock investments. Most brokerages and almost all DRIP plans will allow you to automatically reinvest your dividends to purchase more shares of stock at a low fee or at no fees thus compounding your investment.

REFERENCES

PERIODICALS:
    Investor's Business Daily (newspaper)
    Wall Street Journal (newspaper)
    Value Line Investment Survey (usually available at your public library)

BOOKS
    Buying Stocks Without A Broker by Charles B. Carlson, CFA
    How To Buy Stocks by Uugel and Bond
    One Up On Wall Street by Peter Lynch
    Take On The Street by Arthur Levitt
    The America's Finest Companies Investment Plan by Bill Staton
    The Wealthy Barber by David Chilton
    Winning The Investment Marathon by H. Bradlee Perry

MISCELLANEOUS
    The Motley Fool (on the Internet)
    The Clearinghouse Direct Purchase Plans, 17 State Street, NY, NY 10004
    (source of DRIP plans)
    Yahoo.com-finanancial section
    Scottrade, (Inexpensive online brokerage)

FINANCIAL STATEMENT

You may need to produce a financial statement when you apply for a loan, especially a mortgage loan. A financial statement is a listing of your total assets and debts with your net worth calculated from these two components. I recommend that you do a financial statement once yearly to see where you stand financially. You can use the following information to write down the numbers on a legal pad.

Assets:
Included in assets would be the following examples:
    Cash on hand
    All bank account balances
    CD's
    Bonds
    Equities/Stocks
        (To calculate equity/stock value, multiply the number of shares owned by the closing price for the day of the statement. Ex: Atmos Energy, 20 shares @ $25.00 per share =$500.00.)

Other assets: Usually those assets that you own that have value, but could not immediately be turned in to cash.

    Home (current appraised value)
    Other real estate owned (farm, rent property, etc,)

Household possessions: Use "fire sale" values; do not try to inflate the value of these items. Be realistic in your appraisal.

Automobiles: Again current realistic value. See Kelley's Blue Book for values, available free on-line.

Life Insurance current cash value.

401K and any other retirement plan that you have attained a vested interest in the cash value.

Add your assets to get a total of your possessions.

Liabilities (debts)

Included as liabilities would be the following examples:

Home mortgage (principal only)

Other loans (balance of principal)

Credit card debt

Any other debts (IOU's, time payment loans, etc) (principal only)

Add your liabilities to get a total of your debts.

Now subtract the total liabilities from the total assets to get your net worth.

Total Assets – Total Liabilities = Net Worth

When you are starting out your Net Worth may be a low or negative number, but if truly live within your income, your Net Worth will grow towards the positive over time.

GENERAL SUGGESTIONS

Below is a list of random suggestions in no particular order that reinforce the text above and give you individual ideas that may help you sort out your financial life. You may not be able or willing to take advantage of all suggestions. For that matter you may not be able to afford all of them. However, you can use some of the suggestions to save money and improve your finances.

1. Establish your checking account, savings account and rainy day savings first.
2. If you choose to buy individual stocks, be sure to diversify into different areas of business, not just in one or two stocks. This is the hard part of individual stock holding for the small investor, but can be accomplished through DRIP plans.
3. If you choose to buy mutual funds, you only need two to three funds to cover the necessary investing areas. More funds do not equal more money. This is where you can concentrate your money, the fund provides the diversification.
4. Start investing early in life. Even if you only have $25.00 per month, and increase it as you become, hopefully more financially stable and your income grows. Investors make two major mistakes. They give up in the early stages because they feel that their account will never add up to any significant amount, and secondly each time they do accumulate a significant nest egg they blow it on stuff. New

car, new boat, etc. You are usually you own worst enemy when it comes to investing.

5. This publication is only a quick read introduction to break the ice on investing. Additional reading may be helpful but it not necessary for success. Seek out good advice, and do not mind paying for it. You usually get what you pay for.

6. For those willing to spend a little more time in study, DRIP plans are a good, low cost (in most cases) method of investing for the small investor. With most plans you can take advantage of low fees, dollar cost averaging, automatic investing, and reinvestment of dividends. If you are qualified, many plans offer IRA's. Do not assume because a stock offers a DRIP plan that it is a good investment, or a good plan. Do your research and be sure to check out all fees involved.

7. Dump credit card debt, especially if you have a high rate of interest. The only difference in armed robbery and these high interest cards are (especially if you wind up making only minimum payments) no weapon is used and you volunteer to be robbed monthly.

8. Check with credit reporting agencies every few years to see if bad dept is erroneously reported on your credit report. Some states are starting to force these companies to be more consumer friendly regarding access to these reports.

9. If you are not receiving a statement or report of earnings from the Social Security agency, get a "Request for Statement of Earnings" from your local Social Security office, fill it out and mail it in. You will receive a report in several weeks that informs you if your Social Security account is being properly credited for your employment earnings. There is no guarantee that any of us will ever get anything out of Social Security, but make sure your account is correct just in case there is any money left when you retire.

10. Your car and home are, for the average wage earner, not investments; they are liabilities. Your car and house require payments and interest that suck up a significant portion of most family's earnings. They require constant maintenance and even though your house may go up in value, you have to take out the amount of increase in value that was only the effect of inflation. If your house is an investment, are you going to sell off a bedroom for income when you retire?

11. KISS: Keep it simple stupid! Set out with a reasonable plan, with dollar amount you can stick with over time, start now and stay with it. Do not waste your time with the market being up or down. There is nothing you can do about it anyway.

12. Extended warranties: Ever wonder why the company that sold you your vacuum cleaner calls you at night and informs you that it is almost out of factory warranty, and out of the goodness of their hearts are willing to extend that warranty for a payment? Wake up! They make millions on suckers like you. If you take that money and invest if for yourself you will be better off in the long run. You will find when you get your financial house in order and have back up savings, that these warranties prey on people that do not have their financial houses in order and are afraid that they cannot afford to repair or replace the insured item if it breaks. It is a form of extortion used against the poor and the ignorant.

13. If you receive a bonus, income tax refund or other unexpected income, invest it. You were not expecting the money to begin with, or need it for monthly expenses so do not miss the opportunity to set it aside.

14. Lotteries are for suckers. Only the state wins.

15. Monthly fees are one of the primary moneymakers for companies. How much are you spending monthly on bank accounts, pagers, cell phones, cable service, and extended warranties. etc? Add it up. What services could you trim to have some money to invest? Can anyone really watch 300 TV channels?

16. What other expenses could you curtail to have some money to invest? How many times a month do you eat out or go shopping just for stuff?

17. Keep your car for as long as you can. When a car is paid for, you can use those payments to invest, or to set aside money for the purchase of another car. Yes you will have to pay to maintain the vehicle, but when you compare the cost of a $2,000.00 transmission versus 6 years of payments on a new car, the transmission looks pretty cheap!

18. Pay your bills when they come in the door. This is living on "real money". It will reflect reality in your checkbook reducing the temptation to blow money you do not really have. By paying your

bills on time you will also establish a good credit rating and avoid late fees.

19. Take advantage of programs such as the Defensive Driving Course. You can receive significant savings on your automobile insurance and may actually learn to be a safer driver. After all, if you do become financially successful how much fun will you have spending it from a wheel chair after a bad wreck? As far as this goes, just obey the traffic laws. You will be a safer driver, avoid tickets, wrecks, and increased insurance premiums (money you could invest) and may live longer. It does not matter who is at fault in a wreck, both party's lose.

20. Do not impulse spend. Stop and think about what you are purchasing. If you need to replace an appliance, TV, etc in your home, shop around for the best deal. After all, it is not how much money you make; it is how much money you spend. You can only save the money you do not blow on other expenses. Remember the example of the man that never made over $14,000.00 per year but died with $70,000,000.00

21. On international investing. For the small investor it is usually best to use mutual funds for a small portion, not over 15% of your portfolio to invest in foreign stocks. Some foreign stocks are listed on stock exchanges in America as "ADR's" that are bought and sold just like any other American company but be aware that full disclosure of all information by the company, and access to information about the company may be hard to obtain. Although these stocks have to meet certain requirements to be listed on one of our exchanges, they do not have to meet all the SEC requirements that American companies must meet.

22. If you are married and especially if you have children you need to have a simple will drawn up. This protects you and makes sure your wishes are followed should you die, especially if the children are minors. This is a small expense to protect you, your wife and your children.

23. When making purchases of relatively expensive items (relative to your income) purchase one at a time. This allows you to focus your payments on this item to pay it off in a shorter period of time. You

will save interest, build your credit rating and leave room for error in case another unexpected expense arises.

24. The ROTH IRA is a good investment vehicle, especially if you are unqualified for the standard IRA due to income limits. Due to the tax advantages and access to your money in case of an emergency, this may be the best place for your money once you have reached the "employer matching limit" in your 401K plan. This is certainly the best option, after your 401K plan for your long term investing such are retirement savings. It has the advantage that it avoids all the complicated withdrawal features of the standard IRA plan after age 59 and ½.

GLOSSARY

This list is not a complete list by any means. I have attempted to include some of the terms commonly heard on the news, and used in the financial publications to help you understand what you are reading.

ADR: American depository receipt. This is the form in which you can conveniently purchase some foreign stocks in America. They trade on the principal exchanges.

AMEX: An acronym for the American Stock Exchange.

Analyst: A person who is supposed to have expertise in the evaluation of the finances and potential of investments, such as stocks.

Annuity: A contract purchased from an insurance or mutual fund company that may be paid for in installments or as a single or multiple cash payments. The purpose of an annuity is to provide, under the conditions of the policy, or at your retirement a stream of income over a set period of time or for the rest of your life. There are too many types of annuities to explain in a glossary.

Arbitrage: Buying a stock or other commodity in one market and selling it immediately in another market pocketing the difference in price. Usually done by companies or individuals purchasing large amounts of a stock or commodity and selling it for a small difference in price letting the total profit add up to a significant sum.

Bear market: A period of time in the stock market where the overall prices of stocks decline.

Bid price: The highest price a buyer is willing to offer for a stock.

Bond: A bond is a contract between and individual or other investment entity and a business (company) in which the bondholder agrees to loan the company a set amount of money over a (usually) fixed amount of time. In return the business promises, in the United States normally, to pay interest to the individual at the pre agreed rate twice yearly. At maturity the business agrees to return the principal in full to the individual.

Book Value (of a stock): The sum total of all assets of a company divided by the number of outstanding shares.

Broker: A person that represents a firm that deals in stocks and other securities.

Brokerage: A firm that handles the buying and selling of stocks, bonds and other investments for their customers.

Bull market: A stock market where the overall prices of stocks are increasing over time.

Capital gain/loss: The increase or decrease in the value of the principal of an investment.

CD: Certificate of Deposit. This is an agreement where you loan a bank, a set amount of money for a fixed period of time. The bank agrees to pay you a set amount of interest for the privilege of using your money over that period of time.

Churning: An illegal practice where a broker encourages an investor to buy and sell stocks frequently in his/her account producing a profit for the broker.

Common stock: Fractional ownership in a company that gives you claim to any dividends paid by the company and to any capital gains from appreciation in stock price. Your liability is limited to the amount paid for the stock.

Compounding: Leaving your earning from an investment invested in that investment allowing your principal and your earnings to earn interest/dividends over time.

Deflation: The decrease in the price of goods and services over time thus reflecting an increase in the value of money.

Dividend: The distribution of a payment in stock or cash by a company to holders of common or preferred stock In America, usually paid quarterly on common stock.

Dividend reinvestment: The use of cash dividends paid to you to purchase more shares of the underlying stock in place of taking a cash payment, compounding your investment.

Dividend yield: The dividend in dollars divided by the price of the stock in dollars giving a percent yield. If a stock had a price of $100.00 and paid a $5.00 dividend per year ($1.25/quarter) that would be a 5% dividend yield.

Diversification: Not having all your eggs in one basket. You should not have all your money invested in one, or even a few stocks. You need to have diversity (stocks, some bonds, CD's, cash) as a small investor. This is why mutual funds are a good idea for the small investor. It is the simplest way to attain diversification in many areas.

Dollar Cost Averaging: The best investing method for the small investor. It takes the emotions out of investing, allows you to take advantage of the market's ups and downs, and forces you to invest regularly. It is simply investing regularly (monthly) in a mutual fund or other investment and forgetting about the market fluctuations. Over time it usually works to your advantage.

Dow indexes: There are many Dow indexes representing many of the different business areas. The most commonly quoted is the Dow 30 consisting of some of the primary blue chip companies in America.

EPS: Earnings per share. The amount of earnings of a company divided by the total number of shares.

Equities: Common stock.

FDIC: Federal Deposit Insurance Company. This governmental agency was established during the depression to guarantee the safety, up to specified limits, of deposits in qualified banks of depositors. A similar agency (FSLIC) was set up for savings and loan companies.

Index: There are probably hundreds of different market indexes. These are groups of stocks that have factors in common that allow them to represent the return in a certain market area.

Inflation: The increase of the price of goods and services over time. The "CPI" or consumer price index is one common measure of inflation.

Interest: Money paid for the use of another person's money.

IRA – traditional: A tax deferred investment plan, now limited to individuals that fall under certain income limits.

IRA Roth: A tax deferred investment plan available to most investors in which you invest with after tax dollars, and the principal is allowed to grow tax deferred.

Fiat currency: A system, such as the United States and most other countries today, where the money is declared by governmental decree to be valuable for payment of debts. There is no gold, silver or other underlying asset backing the money. Yeah, that's right, your money is worth nothing!

Liquidity: The ease with which an asset can be converted into cash.

Margin: Using your stocks as collateral to borrow money to purchase more stocks. Most brokerages offer margin accounts.

Market spread, or Spread: The difference in the bid and asked prices of a stock at any given time.

Municipal Bond: A bond issued by a governmental agency that is usually exempt from state and or federal taxes.

Mutual fund: A company that pools the money of many investors and invests these funds for the investors supposedly following the guidelines set out in their prospectus. The service they are selling is management of your money.

NASDAQ: An acronym for National Association of Security Dealers and Automated Quotation Systems. This system handles stock transactions in the "over-the-counter market".

NYSE: An acronym for the New York Stock Exchange also called the "Big Board". Overall it is viewed as having more established companies in its listings. The companies have to meet certain standards to be listed on the NYSE. Again, this does not mean they are good investments< just that they met those standards.

OTC Market: This is actually not a "market" like he NYSE but refers primarily to the stocks traded on the NASDAQ. Some of the smallest stocks that are thinly traded are listed on the "Pink Sheets".

Odd lot trading: Purchasing or selling quantities of stock in numbers other than even lots of 100 (with some exceptions).

PE: Price to earnings ratio - the price per share of the stock divided by the earnings per share of the stock. It is a tool used to compare the performance of one company in a similar business area to another company. For example if bank stocks have an average PE of 10 and your stock has a PE of 12, it is relatively overpriced compared to the market average. It is only an investment tool to be taken in to account with many other factors when making investment decisions.

Pink Sheets: This is a listing of OTC (over the counter) stocks. Many are "penny stocks" meaning that they trade for small sums per share. They are so thinly traded that they are not commonly listed in the NASDAQ listings. Most of these stocks are gambling not investing.

Portfolio: A term that means the overall mix of investment held by a person or company primarily consisting of stocks, bonds, short term investments such as CD's and cash.

Preferred stock: Stocks that really are more bond like in nature. They <u>usually</u> trade in a very tight trading range but offer, usually, high dividend yields compared to the common stock. They have no purpose in the small investor's portfolio.

Prime rate: This represents the interest rate that banks will loan money to their most credit worthy customers. It use used as a base on which to set other loan interest rates. Reported in the business pages of most large newspapers daily.

REIT: Real Estate Investment Trust. These are companies that either purchase real estate or hold mortgages on real estate or a combination of both. They usually have high dividends because the law requires them to distribute most of their income to the shareholders.

Risk: The relative stability of an investment.

Round lot: Buying or selling in even quantities of 100 shares of stock. In some cases other than 100 shares.

S&P 500: A commonly used market index composed of 500 large blue chip companies used to indicate the overall movements of the market.

Spin off: A company decides to split off a particular business segment of the company into another company with it's own stock listing. Usually the parent company spins off the company by distributing shares of the new company to holders of the parent company in proportional shares.

Stock Split: A stock (for example) selling for $100.00 divides each share of stock into two shares worth $50.00 each. It does not change the value of the stock in any way. It is usually used to keep the stock within a "trading range" that makes it easier for small investors to purchase these stocks. If there were no stock splits, some shares of stocks that have done well over the last 100 or so years would be trading for millions of dollars per share. Obviously that would hinder the market.

Tax deferred: Not to be confused with tax-free. It means the government is allowing you to defer the payment of taxes until a later date, allowing you to draw interest/dividends/capital gains on your money over time.

Ticker symbol: Each stock listed on the many stock exchanges is represented by an abbreviation that is used in the financial community to represent that stock. These can be found in most newspaper's stock listings.

Venture Capital: Money put up by investors to fund new companies. Also called in some cases Angel Investors.

SYNOPSIS

If you were already an informed investor and had your financial house in order, you would probably not have purchased this publication. If you are, like the majority of individuals that need help getting their financial house in order I sincerely hope this publication gives you some ideas that help you. You may never have the income to take advantage of all the suggestions incorporated into this text. That does not stop you from using those that you can afford.

Being financially successful does not mean being filthy rich. It means you are in control of your finances and have established a financial plan for life and have the fortitude to stick with it. A good plan will help take the financial strain out of life so you can enjoy yourself. There are millions of excuses why you cannot start today, and millions of reasons to give up if you do ever get started. Many give up, but most never start. Have faith in yourself.

This is the end of this book but it can be the beginning of a new financial life for you. Take one step and a time.

_____

_____

_____

_____

_____

www.ingramcontent.com/pod-product-compliance
Lightning Source LLC
Chambersburg PA
CBHW022133170526
45157CB00004B/1859